making change
for students

PHIL MCMICHAEL
WITH KEN HEMPHILL

Auxano
PRESS

Tigerville, South Carolina

ISBN 978 0 615 19788 3

Quotations in the daily assignments are taken from Making Change: A Transformational Guide to Christian Money Management by Ken Hemphill (Nashville: B&H Publishing Group, 2006).

To order additional copies of these resources, Ken Hemphill, Auxano Press; P.O. Box 315; Tigerville, South Carolina 29688.

For additional resources for this study, go to www.auxanopress.com or contact Ken Hemphill, Auxano Press; P.O. Box 315; Tigerville, South Carolina 29688.

Printed in the United States of America.

CONTENTS

INTRODUCTION

If you are anything like the average teenager, the next six weeks of your life will be filled with drama about relationships, pressure to excel, tension within your family, and questions inside your head about what you can do to make life make more sense. Even if you were going to do an extended Bible study, the last one you think you need right now is one telling you how to manage your money. You might not sign up for that even if you had money, but since you barely have enough to pay for a movie ticket this weekend, this is definitely not something you need right now. Right?

Before you answer that, consider this: what we do with our possessions says volumes about what is most important in our lives. It doesn't matter how much you have. (Just look at the lady who put one penny in the offering plate in Mark, chapter 12.) What matters is what you do with what God gives you, and what habits you start now that will influence how you use your possessions later. Will you really trust Him now to be the Lord of every part of your life, even your possessions?

So, back to the insane life of a teenager -- is it possible that in the middle of the craziness of life, God may want to show you how to get through it better by doing a study about money? It is said that God's Scripture is His love letter to His people. If one of the topics He talks about most in that letter is money, then maybe studying what He says about it will help you to understand just a little more of how He plans to bring you peace and purpose right in the middle of your pressure-filled life.

As you begin this study, you will find that this member book is divided into seven weekly sections with the following components:

- *Viewer guide.* Each week begins with a page for you to record notes as you watch the DVD during your group session.

- *Group discussion guide.* These pages will guide you through the group session. If you are studying on your own, take the time to read the Scriptures and to think about the questions asked. You can record your thoughts on these pages or the notes page.

- *Daily study.* Five daily readings each week provide questions to guide you in examining your approach to money management and in aligning your practices with God's stewardship plan for His people.

Right now, set a goal of when you are going to do this study each day – right before school, right after school, right after dinner – you choose a good time for you. Try to set aside fifteen minutes every weekday for the next month and a half. That may seem like a lot, but really, we could all spare fifteen minutes from TV, web surfing, or video games. Plus, when you think about it, isn't ten or fifteen minutes a day worth trading in for a little clearer perspective on life?

AUTHORS

PHIL McMICHAEL

Phil McMichael holds a Masters of Divinity from New Orleans Baptist Theological Seminary, and a degree in education from Louisiana Tech University. He has worked in the student ministry since 1995, serving in churches in Germantown, Tennessee; Shreveport, Louisiana; and Amite, Louisiana. Currently, Phil serves as the Student Discipleship Pastor at Prestonwood Baptist Church, Plano, Texas.

KEN HEMPHILL

Kingdom giving and kingdom living are important to author Ken Hemphill. Dr. Hemphill is the National Strategist for Empowering Kingdom Growth of the Southern Baptist Convention. He holds a Ph.D. from Cambridge University and is the former president of Southwestern Baptist

Theological Seminary. Other video-driven resources by Ken Hemphill include *EKG: The Heartbeat of God, Making Change: A Transformational Guide to Christian Money Management* and *The Prayer of Jesus*. Other books include *Parenting with Kingdom Purpose,* and the Kingdom Promises devotional series.

God's Design for Managing Money

1. Where does God's design for managing money begin?

"In the beginning _____..." *Genesis 1:21*

2. How should we respond to God as Creator?

"Though they knew God, they did not glorify Him as God or show _____." *Romans 1:21*

3. What's the difference between being an owner and a steward?

Ownership creates _____.

4. How does God's plan of salvation/redemption relate to money and material possessions?

"The ground is cursed because of you. You will eat from it by means of painful _____ all the days of your life. It will produce thorns and thistles for you, and you will eat the plants of the field. You will eat bread by the sweat of your brow until you return to the ground, since you were taken from it. For you are dust, and you will return to dust.
Genesis 3:17-19

The earth and everything in it, The world and its inhabitants, Belong to the Lord. Psalm 24:1

one

God's Design for Managing Money

Name something you regularly use today that you didn't have five years ago.

Did you have to change to begin to use this item? How?

How has using this item changed you?

What do you think making change means?

Can you think of more than one meaning? Write your thoughts.

Turn to the viewer guide on page 9 and record your responses as you watch this week's DVD segment.

1. The Beginning Read Genesis 1:1, 26-31.

God told Adam and Eve that everything He had created was theirs to care for, rule, and subdue.

God spoke: "Let us make human beings in our image, make them reflecting our nature so they can be responsible for the fish in the sea, the birds in the air, the cattle, and yes, Earth itself, and every animal that moves on the face of the Earth." God created human beings; he created them godlike, reflecting God's nature. He created them male and female. God blessed them: "Prosper! Reproduce! Fill Earth! Take charge! Be responsible for the fish in the sea and birds in the air, for every living thing that moves on the face of Earth."

Genesis 1:26-28, *The Message*

What do you think these verses mean for Christians today?

2. God, Our Creator Read Romans 1:20-21.

God, our Creator, is the source of everything we are and have. Romans 1:21 tells us that _____ is the appropriate response.

3. Owner or Steward? Read Matthew 6:19-21, 25-34.

Jesus said we should not _____ about what we will eat or wear. How does thinking of God as owner and yourself as His steward affect your thinking about material goods and your responsibility?

4. God's Redemptive Plan Read Genesis 3:17; Romans 8:20-25.

In Genesis 1 God gave Adam and Eve work to do. In Genesis 3, because of their sins, God said that work would now be difficult. But the coming of Christ brought God's plan of redemption. Paul wrote in Romans that all the earth will one day overcome the effects of sin and be fully restored to God's divine plan.

God's redemptive plan should affect everything we do. As a Christ-follower, how does God's gift of salvation affect –

the way you view your work?

the way you view your place in God's kingdom?

your responsibility for others?

your responsibility for being a steward of your time, talents, possessions, and money?

What insight have you gained about God's design for managing money?

prayer Talk about what our prayers should look like in regard to today's lesson. Take a minute to write a short prayer about what you've learned.

In the Beginning
God

In the beginning God created
the heavens and the earth. Genesis 1:1

The earth and everything in it,
The world and its inhabitants,
Belong to the Lord;
For He laid its foundation on the seas
And established it on the rivers. Psalm 24:1-2

Starting with the first sentence of the Bible, "In the beginning, God," God is the subject of the Bible. God's creation, including man, is here for Him and because of Him. We tend to get that backwards. In our minds we are the center of the universe. We think that God should be here for us, not that our lives should exist to glorify Him. This idea sets up the basic conflict in life – will I put myself first, or will I give God His rightful place, in charge of me and the world and everything in it?

Before you convince yourself that is not true, take a second to answer the following questions:

Do you try to please your parent(s)? Why?

Do you try to make good grades? Why?

When you are not doing school work and are not at church, how do you spend your time? Why do you do those things?

For most students, the answers to these questions all point to self. We want to please our parents because we love them, but we also know that a happy parent can mean freedom and rewards for us. We may or may not like studying, but we also know that good grades now mean better financial opportunities later. Our free time activities may involve other people, but usually they are things that bring us love or attention or laughs or satisfaction or maybe even all four.

Even though your life may be about you, creation is about God. The guy who wrote Psalm 50 for God got it right when he said:

> Every animal of the forest is Mine,
> The cattle on a thousand hills.
> I know every bird of the mountains,
> And the creatures of the field are mine.

Your focus may be on your life, but everything you have belongs to God – your home, your iPod, your family, your talents, your dress clothes, your gym bag, and your favorite t shirt. He may allow you to have those things for your enjoyment, but His primary purpose for providing you with everything you have is to give you the opportunity to glorify His name.

Bring glory to God

How can you bring glory to God with the following things:

iPod

biggest hobby

biggest talent

relationships with family

clothes

time on computer

friendships

job

Read Psalm 95:3-6. Write a similar poem that praises God for the parts of His creation that you have seen or experienced. Once you finish, talk to Him using that poem as your prayer.

Go to the *Week One Wrap-Up* on page 22 and write down one idea or Scripture that stood out to you today.

day
two

It Was
Very Good

God saw all that He had made, and it was very good.
Genesis 1:31

Throughout the first chapter of Genesis we see God repeating His thoughts of the "good-ness" of His creation. As He created light, and the seas, and dry land, and vegetation, and animals, and birds and man, He could stand back and see that each part of His creation was good.

Not all religions see the physical world or material possessions as good, but throughout the Bible we see a repetition of this idea of the creation's goodness.

Ecclesiastes 3:11 states,
"He [God] has made everything beautiful in its time." (NIV)

James 1:17 says,
"Every good and perfect gift is from above, coming down from the Father of the heavenly lights, who does not change like shifting shadows." (NIV)

1 Timothy 4:4 writes,
"Everything created by God is good." (NIV)

If all of God's creation is good, why do you think the Bible has so many warnings in it about our possessions?

Look up the following two verses and write down what they are warning against:

Romans 1:25

Matthew 6:24

The danger we face with our possessions is that we will care about the things God created more than we will care about God Himself.

Self – Check Up

If your family and friends looked at the way you spend your time and money, what would they think are the top three most important things in your life?

1) _____

2) _____

3) _____

What other evidence would you give that God is the One you serve?

God has given us the ability to experience His creation and to know that it is good. Think about the past 24 hours and fill in the blanks below.

Today I saw _____, and it was good.

Today I heard _____, and it was good.

Today I tasted _____, and it was good.

Today I touched _____, and it was good.

Today I smelled _____, and it was good.

If you could not fill in every blank, then you are not enjoying God's creation the way He planned. Even in the midst of tough times in our lives, the goodness of God's creation is designed to point us to Him so that our lives may be more fulfilling. When you choose to be aware of God's creation and what God does for those who call Him Lord, you'll react the way Peter and John did:

"We are unable to stop speaking about what we have seen and heard" (Acts 4:20).

Look back at the blanks you filled in about your last 24 hours. Spend some time thanking God for the blanks you did fill in. Ask God to help you enjoy His creation more the rest of this week. Ask Him to help you to be more aware of Him as you enjoy it.

Go to the *Week One Wrap-Up* on page 22 and write down one idea or Scripture that stood out to you today.

day
three

Created in His Image

God said, "Let us make man in Our image, according to Our likeness. They will rule the fish of the sea, the animals, all the earth, and the creatures that crawl on the earth." Genesis 1:26

The phrases "in Our image" and "according to Ours likeness" found in Verse 26 speak volumes about God's intention for our lives. How do you think mankind reflects God's image or likeness? (Compare us to the rest of creation if you need to.)

Your image

If you were made in God's image, what do you think this says about God's plan for your life?

God's appointment to Adam and Eve in Genesis 1 makes them both responsible and accountable for the management of His creation. We know that the Bible warns us about valuing the creation more than the Creator. However, because Genesis 1 shows us that part of God's purpose for us is to protect and manage His creation, we should be more concerned than anyone about our care for God's natural resources.

What are some ways that God's creation is being harmed by mankind?

Read 1 Corinthians 4:2. What does God require of a steward, or manager?

What can you begin doing right now to take better care of
His creation?

What are some things you can do when you become an adult as a
response to God's plan for you to care for creation?

Take a moment to thank God for His creation. Ask Him to begin
showing you small ways you can be a better manager of His creation
right now.

Go to the *Week One Wrap-Up* on page 22 and write down one idea or
Scripture that stood out to you today.

day four

The Impact of the Fall

*The ground is cursed because of you.
You will eat of it by means of painful labor
all the days of your life. Genesis 3:17*

When we allow wealth to become our god, we are rewarded by anxiety and uneasiness. We are doomed to spend our time taking care of our god, protecting it from moth, rust, and thieves. The choice is pretty clear: we can either choose to serve God who can take care of [us], or we can spend our days anxiously taking care of the god of our own making.

Making Change, page 23

Genesis 3:17 shows us just one of the results of the fall of man. Also because of the fall, God's good gifts to us now provide opportunities for ongoing sin. Put a check mark beside any of these that you have struggled with lately.

___ We try to get as much cool stuff as possible for ourselves, instead of looking for ways that we can provide for others who are really in need.

___ We try to be friends with some people because of what they can give us or do for us.

___ We let hobbies, things and people (the creation) become more important to us than God.

Read 1 Kings 21:1-4. How is Ahab's attitude similar to how many people view possessions today?

In the end of this story, Ahab and his wife have Naboth killed so that they can have his vineyard. How is this similar to the way we desire to collect many possessions and clothes when we know that there are people who are dying around the world because they do not have money for food?

Impact of the Word
Write out Matthew 6:13.

How does this verse apply to what you have read today?

What is one thing you think you should pray in regards to Matthew 6:13 and the rest of today's lesson?

Take a few moments to talk to God about your feelings for possessions. Ask God to help you to please Him with any possessions He gives you. Ask Him to show you ways you can help others with your possessions. Ask Him to help you to care more about ministering to others than you do about gaining more possessions.

Go to the *Week One Wrap-Up* on page 22 and write down one idea or Scripture that stood out to you today.

day five

Redemption and the Material World

Put on the new self, created to be like God
in true righteousness and holiness. Ephesians 4:24 (NIV)

Read Romans 10:9. To be saved, what must a person do?

If you really do desire and need Christ to be the Lord of your entire life, how should that affect your worldly possessions?

Read Luke 19:1-9. What was the evidence that Zacchaeus had made Christ the Lord of his life?

If a homeless person could see how you spend your money (and your parents' money), what would that person think is the lord, or most important thing, in your life?

Salvation does not just change our eternal destination; it changes everything. Have you made Christ the Lord of your life – all of your life?

If you have not yet entered into a personal relationship with Jesus Christ, you can make this wonderful discovery today. Let's use the acrostic **LIFE** to explain how you can inherit eternal life and also experience earthly life to its fullest.

Love
God created you in His image. You were created to live in relationship with Him.
"For God so loved the world in this way: He gave His One and Only
Son, so that everyone who believes in Him will not perish
but have eternal life (John 3:16).

Isolation
Isolation from God is caused by our sin, our rebellion against God. It separates us from Him and from others.
"For all have sinned and fall short of the glory of God" (Romans 3:23)

Forgiveness
The only solution to our isolation and separation from holy God is forgiveness.
"For Christ also suffered for sins once for all, the righteous for the
unrighteous, that he might bring you to God (1 Peter 3:18).

The only way our relationship can be restored with God is through the forgiveness of our sins. Jesus Christ died on the cross for this very purpose.

Eternal life – You can have full and abundant life in this present life and eternal life when you die.

"But to all who did receive Him, He gave them the right to be children of God, to those who believe in his name" (John 1:12).

"A thief comes only to steal and to kill and to destroy. I have come that they may have life and have it in abundance" (John 10:10).

All you have to do is:

Admit that you are a sinner. Turn away from your sin and turn to Jesus as Lord of your life.

Believe that Jesus died for your sins and rose from the dead.

Confess verbally and publicly your belief in Jesus Christ.

You can invite Jesus into your life right now by praying something like this: "God, I admit that I am a sinner. I believe You sent Jesus to die on the cross to pay the penalty for my sins. And I believe that God raised Him from the dead. I am asking You to forgive me of my sin. In Jesus' name I ask for this gift. Amen."

If you have a friend or family member who is a Christian, tell them about your decision. Then find a church where you can learn more about Jesus and the life He wants you to have.

Galatians 4:7 says

"You are no longer a slave, but a son; and since you are a son, God has made you also an heir." (NIV)

Because you have put your faith in Jesus for salvation, God now considers you a child of His. As His child, will you let Him help you to make changes to give Him control of your possessions? If there are some things that you are afraid to make available to God for His use, write those things down.

Go to the *Week One Wrap-Up* on the next page and write down any commitment you made today. If you didn't make any commitment, write down one idea or Scripture that stood out to you today.

wrap-up

Day One Thought or Verse

Day Two Thought or Verse

Day Three Thought or Verse

Day Four Thought or Verse

Day Five Commitment, Thought or Verse

As a result of this week's study, one area of my life that I need to pray more about is:

One goal I would like to set as a result of this week's study:

One commitment I am making this week is to:

two

The Purpose Of Money

1. What is the purpose of money?

To meet our _____

To give us _____

To _____ with those in need

To expand _____

To _____ the nations

2. How does obedience relate to money?

"When you eat and are full, you will _____ the Lord your God for the good land He has given you." Deuteronomy 8:10

God gives us His provision, protection, and _____.

3. According to the Bible, what are the dangers of money and material possessions?

To confirm His _____

> You may say to yourself, "My power and my own ability have gained this wealth for me," but remember that the Lord your God gives you the power to gain wealth, in order to confirm His covenant He swore to your fathers, as it is today.
> Deuteronomy 8:17-18

4. What does Jesus teach about the meaning of money and material goods?

God wants us to:

1. Embody His _____.

2. Embrace His _____.

3. Obey His _____.

Money can create earthly _____ or _____ investment.

two

The Purpose Of Money

Share what God taught you this past week. Share any goals or commitments you made.

Think of the ways you use money. Name four categories.

1. _____   3. _____

2. _____   4. _____

How does having or not having money affect your day-to-day life?

How does it affect your habits and outlook on life?

Can you imagine a society without money? How would it function?

Turn to the viewers guide on page 23. Record your responses as you watch the DVD segment by segment. Between segments, discuss your answers.

1. The Purpose of Money

All the ways you use money can be summarized as: spend it, give it away, save it, and invest it. But the ways you use money are different from the purposes of money.

Ken Hemphill names four purposes of money. List them here:

1. _____   3. _____

2. _____   4. _____

How does the way you use money affect your ability to fulfill God's purposes for money and material goods?

2. Obedience and Blessing Read Deuteronomy 8.

Obedience to God and receiving His blessings are directly related. What happened 40 years earlier when the Hebrew people did not obey God?

How many times in Deuteronomy 8 are the people told to obey God?

How does the passage specifically relate obedience to wealth?

God's blessings include His protection, His provision, and His presence. How are these three types of blessings evident in Deuteronomy 8?

Do you think wealthy people today are obedient to God? If not, how do you interpret Deuteronomy 8 in our society today?

3. Warning! Look again at Deuteronomy 8:17-18.

How does God make clear that He is the source of all people need?

What is the warning, or danger, in gaining wealth?

What can we do today to heed this warning and to avoid the pitfall of thinking we are responsible for our own success?

If God is the source of all we have, what is our role or responsibility in gaining or earning money!

4. Jesus' View

How does the Lord's Prayer include the responses God wants?

1. Embody His name _____

2. Embrace His mission _____

3. Obey His Word _____

How does the prayer address God's protection, provision, and presence?

What other teachings of Jesus relate to money, wealth, or material possessions? How does each relate to what we read in Deuteronomy 8?

prayer Close by saying the Lord's Prayer together.

day one

God's Heartbeat

When you eat and are full, you will praise the Lord
your God for the good land He has given you.
Deuteronomy 8:10

The earth and everything in it,
The world and its inhabitants,
Belong to the Lord;
For He laid its foundation on the seas
And established it on the rivers. Psalm 24:1-2

If the blessing of God involves his presence, his provision, and
his protection, then his cursing means man's forfeiture of the
same. It is not so much that God withholds blessing as it is
that we reject it.   *Making Change*, page 35

Read Deuteronomy 8.
Name four ways that this passage says God had already blessed the
Israelites.

Name four ways this passage says God was about to bless the
Israelites.

What are four commands that God gives the Israelites in this
passage?

What did God say would happen if they disobey these commands?
(vs. 14,17,19)

God's warning to the Israelites was that they not forget God as the source of all good gifts. His warning to us is the same today. We need to remember that He provides for us rather than to think that through our efforts, ingenuity, and hard work we have earned or created our wealth, good fortune and success on our own.

Write down your memory of a time when you disobeyed God and suffered consequences that were a result of that act.

What are some ways you are tempted to be disobedient to God with your possessions and abilities?

Write down any other ways that wealth may potentially hurt your relationship with God.

Read Psalm 103:8-10.
Although this passage reminds us of God's patience with us when we make mistakes, Hebrews 12:6 states,

> "the Lord disciplines those he loves, and he punishes everyone he accepts as a son." (NIV)

God's love for us keeps Him from immediately giving us the punishment we deserve when we do things such as taking His gifts for granted and using them only for our pleasure and not for the benefit of His kingdom. On the other hand, His love for us is also the reason that He must discipline us in some way for those things, so that we do not let our possessions keep us from enjoying the close relationship with Him that we need.

> Otherwise ... your heart will become proud and you will forget the Lord your God. Deuteronomy 8:14 (NIV)

On the *Week Two Wrap-Up*, on page 36, write a prayer asking God to draw you closer to Him and thanking Him for His salvation and for the many good gifts He has given to you.

day two

Meeting Needs, Providing Pleasure

My God will supply all your needs according to His riches in glory in Christ Jesus. Philippians 4:19

> The key issue in life is balance. When we talk about material possessions and enjoyment of life, we are really speaking about contentment. *Making Change*, page 40

In one of the lines from a recent hit song the singer, already a millionaire, proclaimed:

> I want a brand new house
> On an episode of Cribs
> And a bathroom I can play baseball in.[1]

The guys who wrote that song aren't the first people to long for more than they can get their hands on. It seems like that need for more, no matter how much or how little we have, has been around forever.

Solomon, who was both wise and wealthy, wrote about wealth and pleasure,

> "I thought in my heart, 'Come now, I will test you with pleasure to find out what is good.' But that also proved to be meaningless" (Eccl. 2:1). (NIV)

Perhaps Solomon's problem – and ours today – is that his life was out of balance. Although God provides for our pleasure, several other points are important to consider.

1.   We are partners with God in our provision. God gives us work to do. God has provided you with gifts, skills, and strengths. If you are not using those to make money already, one day you will. As hard as this may be for you to believe right now, when you partner with God, work can become rewarding and satisfying.

2.   Although God provides for our needs and our pleasure, He wants us to do more than meet our own needs and wants. When we see no farther than our own needs, we limit His purposes for our use of His resources. In other words, God

wants to bring joy to your life by allowing you to help others with the possessions He has given to you. When we are focused on our own selves and desires, we miss out on the satisfaction that comes when God works through our lives to bless others - kind of like Scrooge in that old Christmas movie.

Are You Satisfied?

In Proverbs we read,

"A righteous man eats until he is satisfied" (13:25).

How much do you need to be satisfied?

How would you define enough?

Read Psalm 16:11. What kinds of pleasures do you think the psalmist is thinking about now and in the future?

Write a prayer thanking God for meeting your needs and for giving you pleasure in all He has provided. In that prayer, ask Him to help you to enjoy the satisfaction He wants you to have in what you already have, and not to get stressed out longing for things you don't have.

Go to the *Week Two Wrap-Up* on page 36 and write down one idea or Scripture that stood out to you today.

[1] "Rockstar," Nickelback, The All Blacks B.V. Roadrunner Records, 2007.

day
three

Caring for the Needy

Give to everyone who asks you, and if anyone
takes what belongs to you, do not demand it back.
Luke 6:30 (NIV)

> The clear message of the Old Testament is that God's heart
> beats for the poor, that he reaches out to meet their need,
> and that his preferred way of doing so is to meet their need
> through us – so that the needs of both of us can be met at
> the same time.   *Making Change*, page 44

An inner-city church joined others to prepare small kits of hygiene
essentials for homeless veterans. Students were invited to lead the
way in the project, collecting items for the kits, assembling them, and
writing personal notes for the intended but unknown recipients.

When the kits were complete and ready to deliver, one wise
leader suggested reading the notes before releasing the kits. Students
had been encouraged to write messages like "God loves you, and so
do we." But one of the leaders found this message: "You're lazy. Why
don't you get a job?"

Even though we may not like to work, deep down most of us
know that hard work is necessary. Sometimes that belief causes us
to judge those in need and keeps us from helping them. Regardless
of the possible reasons for a person being poor and needy, we are
accountable for our response to other's needs. In 1 John 3:17 we read,
"If anyone has this world's goods and sees his brother in
need but shuts off his compassion from him—
how can God's love reside in him?"
Basically this verse is saying that, if a person has a relationship with
Christ, that relationship should be evident in the way that person
shows compassion to others in need.

Read Ephesians 4:28. What does Paul say to someone who
won't work?

What do you think is your responsibility as a Christian to help care for the needy? Is your thinking consistent with biblical teaching?

Could there be needy students in your church? List two ways you can show them compassion without drawing attention to yourself or making them feel inferior.

Do you know of any needy teenagers outside of your church? What is one way you can show one of them compassion this week without embarrassing them?

What is one thing your family could sacrifice every month that would free up money for you to help those teens?

If your youth group worked with other area youth groups, what affect could you have on helping the needy in your community?

If the churches in your community worked together, do you think you could meet the needs of all of those less fortunate in your community?
Do you think God is able to provide the funds for you to do that if you all worked together?

Do you think it is possible for Christians worldwide to deal with poverty and the issues that cause poverty?

Read James 2:14-18. How do your actions to those in need give evidence of your faith?

Spend some time asking God to show you steps you can take to help yourself, your church, and your family to be more caring to the needy.

Go to the *Week Two Wrap-Up* on page 36 and write down any steps God may be calling you to take to help others.

day four

Ministry Support and Expansion

The people rejoiced because of their leaders' willingness
to give, for they had given to the Lord with a whole
heart. King David also rejoiced greatly.
1 Chronicles 29:9

> When people begin responding to God's heartbeat, there
> will be more than enough! God will make available through
> us the resources necessary to advance his kingdom.
> *Making Change*, page 50

In Malachi 3:10 God says,
"Bring your full tithe to the Temple treasury so there will
be ample provisions in my Temple" (The Message).
The tithe, which we'll consider in more depth later, is meant for
use through the church. God's instruction directs believers to give
this portion of their belongings to the church. Here are a few of the
instances of God's instruction on giving to the church:

ᕽ Read Exodus 36:3-6. What paid for the construction of the
very first worship sanctuary that is talked about here?

When the people agreed to give, how much do verses 5 & 7 say
they gave?

ᕽ Many years later David, working with Solomon, used his
influence to develop a design for the new temple, to enlist
craftsmen, and to ask the people to give. Again, they gave so
generously that Solomon had more than he needed to build the
temple (see 1 Chron. 22:1-13; 29:6-9).

ᕽ Ministry giving means more than constructing and
maintaining buildings. It also means caring for God's chosen
leaders. In the Old Testament it meant supporting the Levites,
God's chosen priests. In the New Testament Paul wrote to
Timothy that the church should support those who preach
(see 1 Timothy 5:17).

The ministry doesn't end with buildings and staff salaries. Because of tithes and offerings, people hear the good news of Jesus Christ and receive all kinds of Christian ministry in church communities and around the world.

Sometimes people like the idea of giving to a specific cause instead of giving ongoing support to their church. Why is it necessary to give tithes to the church?

How is this consistent with the verses you looked at in today's study?

What would happen if all church members gave their money to specific ministries and good causes instead of giving any to the general budget of their local church?

How would your life change if your church ceased to exist because of a lack of sufficient funds?

Are you giving voluntarily and joyfully to support your church? If not, what is a goal you can set for supporting your local church every week, or at least every month?

Ask God to help you to know how much you should give weekly (or monthly) to your church. Ask Him to use those gifts to bring Him glory and to point people toward His great love.

Go to the *Week Two Wrap-Up* on page 36 and write down one idea or Scripture that stood out to you today.

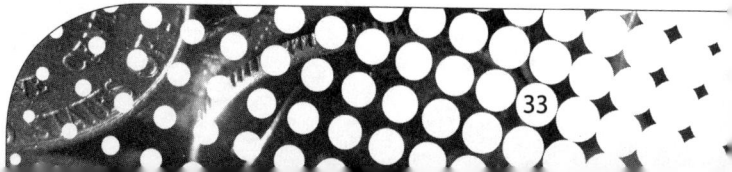

day five

Reaching the Nations

I saw One like the son of man
Coming with the clouds of heaven.
He approached the Ancient of Days
And was escorted before Him.
He was given authority to rule, and glory,
and a kingdom; so that those of every people,
nation, and language should serve Him.
His dominion is an everlasting dominion
that will not pass away, and His kingdom is one
that will not be destroyed. Daniel 7:13-14

When you read that Scripture from Daniel, who does God say will
be around His throne worshiping Him?
We know that God's plan is that the Gospel will reach people from
every nation and every language. If He really desires that to happen,
doesn't it make sense that He would provide the money and resources
needed to spread the Gospel to all nations?

God began communicating His desire that all nations worship Him
in the first book of the Bible. In Genesis 12 God called Abraham to
leave home and to follow Him:

Go out from your land,
Your relatives, And your father's house
To the land that I will show you.
I will make you into a great nation,
I will bless you, I will make your name great,
And you will be a blessing.
I will bless those who bless you,
I will curse those who treat you with contempt,
And all the peoples on earth
Will be blessed through you. Genesis 12:1-3

Circle the lines in that passage that refer to God's plan for all nations
to know Him.

Where did God tell Abram to go in this passage?

There aren't many people who like uncertainty. We like to know how much money we'll have this week so we can know how much we can spend on junk food, how much we can spend on gas, how much we can spend on clothes, and how much we need to save for the weekend. If mom tells you that she will let you know on Friday if she is going to give you money for a movie, that can mess with your head all week. If dad says he won't pay for car insurance next month, your whole life could be jacked.

We just don't like uncertainty. But God's plan is based on faith, not on how much we have or how much we will get; not what we want to do this weekend or what we hope to be doing this summer. God tells us to

> "Bring the best of the first fruits of your land to the house of the Lord your God" (Exodus 23:19).

In this, God is telling us that whenever we gain any possessions, we should first look for a way to use them to bless God.

Bless God

Circle any of the following you plan to get this year:

Christmas money birthday money allowance

money for graduation or good grades salary from work

To reach the nations with the good news of Jesus Christ means that people must go, leaving home as Abram did, not knowing where their journey will take them. It also means that people must give, not knowing what their needs will be tomorrow but trusting God to bless those who go, as well as those who give.

Of God's four purposes for money – meeting your needs and giving you pleasure, caring for the needy, supporting ministry, and reaching the nations – which has been your primary focus in the past?

What changes is God leading you to make in your life in order to use your money for kingdom purposes?

Finish the *Week Two Wrap-Up* on the next page.

35

wrap-up

Day One Prayer

Day Two Thought or Verse

Day Three Question
To help others, God may be calling me to:

Day Four Thought or Verse

Day Five Thought or Verse

As a result of this week's study, one area of my life that I
need to pray more about is:

One goal I would like to set as a result of this
week's study:

three Earning, Spending, Saving, Investing

1. What is whole-life stewardship?

   God is the Creator and _____ of everything?

   God created us in _____ image.

   Material _____ are equally irrelevant in both our entrance into the world and our exit from it.

   Material possessions have meaning when used according to _____'s intention.

   God wants to provide additional resources to those committed to _____ principles.

2. What is God's plan for earning a living?

   Focus on _____.

   Serve with _____.

   Serve with _____ and enthusiasm.

   Serve with _____.

   Learn to _____ with others.

   Be willing to _____.

   Why does a fool have money in his hand with no intention of buying wisdom? Proverbs 17:16

3. What is God's plan for spending?

   Have written _____.

   Know where _____ are.

   Develop a _____.

   Act you w_____.

   Establish a goal for _____ purchases.

4. Is debt ever biblical?

   "The wicked borrows and does not _____, but the righteous is gracious and giving." Psalm 37:21.

Earning, Spending, Saving, Investing

What is one old saying you have heard your parents or other adults say about money?

What lessons have the following taught you about money:
1) School?   2) Friends?
3) Media?   4) Family?

Think of the money you have earned or received in the last month. How much has gone to giving, spending, saving, and investing?

If you could change those percentages, what would be your ideal distribution?

Turn to the viewer guide on page 37 and record your responses as you watch this week's DVD segment. Or complete the viewer guide as you watch the DVD segment by segment for each of the numbered sections that follow.

1. Whole-Life Stewardship Read 1 Kings 3:5-15.

We are taught that Solomon asked for wisdom instead of riches and that God blessed him for his choice. Verse 9 is translated in various ways. Read several versions.

In various translations, what did Solomon ask God to give him?

Reading Solomon's request in several translations gives a clearer picture of what Solomon wanted—a heart like his father, David, who desired to do what God wanted him to do. Have you asked God what He wants you to do with your life? Your money?

Whole-life stewardship means wisely using everything God has given you—time, talents, money, etc.—not just money. And it means that you are accountable for the way you use all your time, talents, money, etc.—not just the amount you give back to God.

What are some ways people are poor stewards of what God has provided, other than money?

What are some ways people can be good stewards of all of life?

2. God's Plan for Earning Read Ecclesiastes 9:10.

With what attitude should a Christian approach work?

God ordained work even before the fall. Read Genesis 1:26-31; 2:15. Work was part of creation, and it was good.

A whole-life stewardship approach to work means that we should: (1) focus on service; (2) serve with excellence; (3) serve with diligence and enthusiasm; (4) serve with integrity.

How might your attitude and effort toward work shift with a whole-life-stewardship approach?

What about your attitude toward school?

3. Spending Read Proverbs 17:16.

If wisdom in this verse means what it did in 1 Kings 3, how would you spend money in obedience to God's desire?

What are some ways that we can discover God's desires for our spending?

4. Debt Read Deuteronomy 15:6-8; Proverbs 22:7; Psalm 112:5; Romans 13:8.

What do these verses teach us about borrowing and lending? Practically, when do you think it is OK to borrow money?

From an obedient, whole-life perspective, when is debt not a good idea?

In the areas of earning, spending, saving, and investing, what specific habit in one of these areas would you like God to help you change?

prayer Partner with someone to pray for each other's concerns.

day one

Whole-life Stewardship

Why does a fool have money in his hand with no intention of buying wisdom? Proverbs 17:16

This is the way I live, lil' boy still pushin' big wheels.
I stack my money lay low and chill;
Don't need to work hard that's the way I feel.
This is the way I live.[1]

You may or may not recognize these lyrics to a popular rap song. As you think about the words to that song, read Luke 12:15-21. Write down any similarities you see between the thoughts in the song and the attitude of the rich man in Luke.

Similarities:

Although their attitude towards work may have differed, both the guy from the song and the rich man from Luke had this in common: they wanted to accumulate all the money they could for themselves and they both left God out of the equation. They needed to be reminded of the truth in Paul's words to Timothy: "we brought nothing into the world, and we can take nothing out" (1 Tim. 6:7)

It can be easy to sometimes think that God is out to get someone who succeeds. Not so. The Bible teaches that God wants to give good gifts to His children. But He also wants His children to understand that everything they have comes from Him. He also wants them to remember that they are accountable for all He supplies – not just the portion they give back to Him.

Malachi 3:10 says,

"Bring the whole tithe into the storehouse, that there may be food in my house. Test me in this," says the Lord God Almighty, "and see if I will not throw open the floodgates of heaven and pour out so much blessing that you will not have room enough for it." (NIV)

What does God want to do for His people? What is preventing this from happening?

Until now you have not asked for anything in my name.
Ask and you will receive, and your joy will be complete.
John 16:24 (NIV)

In whose name should Christians make their appeals to God?

What does this verse reflect as God's desire for His people?

Anytime we think about stewardship, we must think of it in terms of totality – whole life. How can I advance God's kingdom at school? What about at work? At my club? In my home? In my prayer time? How can I work and compete and practice in a way that reflects God's love and His grace?

My Definition
In your words, what is "whole-life stewardship?"

Whole-life Stewardship is…

If you, like Solomon could ask God for one gift, what would it be? Why?

Ask God to help you to be a good steward of every part of your life.

Go to the *Week Three Wrap-Up* on page 50 and write down one idea or Scripture that stood out to you today.

---

[1] "The Way I Live," Baby Boy Da Prince, Universal Records, 2006.

day two

How to Earn Money

What does a man gain for all his efforts he labors at under the sun? Ecclesiastes 1:3

God is the owner, man is the manager, and therefore man's labor is from the hand of God. This principle is as old as the garden. God created the earth and all that is within it, and then He gave man the privilege of cultivating it as His steward. *Making Change*, page 68

* Americans work more hours on average than workers in any other county in the industrialized world.

* American workers are more productive than workers in other countries, but they are not more efficient.

* Every year Americans work more hours and take less vacation than their European counterparts.

* The average Australian, Canadian, Japanese, or Mexican worker was on the job roughly 100 fewer hours than the average American in a year. That's almost 2 ½ weeks less.

Why do you think Americans spend so much time at work?

Why do you think Americans are not more efficient?

Think about the time you spend studying. How could you be more efficient with that time?

Read the following verses and note what they say about God's perspective of work.

Ecclesiastes 9:10

Colossians 3:23

1 Timothy 5:8

Titus 3:14

What are the dangers of making work your primary focus in life?

How should whole-life stewardship affect your schoolwork?

How should it affect your job(s)?

Ask God to help you to honor Him with the way you work.

Go to the *Week Three Wrap-Up* on page 50 and write down one idea or Scripture that stood out to you today.

day
three

How to Spend Money

Why do you spend money on what is not food,
and your wages on what does not satisfy? Isaiah 55:2

> If we don't learn to manage our spending, we will never
> be able to save or to give. Thus, if we ignore the Creator's
> directives in this area of financial management… we will
> continue to rob from God, which in turn robs us from
> experiencing His full blessing.
>
> *Making Change*, pages 74-75

Consider these two statistics:

- ✧ The average size of new single-family homes being built in
  the United States today is 2,227 square feet. That's up from
  1,525 in 1973, an increase of 46 percent.[1]

- ✧ There are about 50,000 self-storage units nationally, double
  the number of a decade ago, according to the national Self-
  Storage Association.[2]

What kinds of things do people put in storage units?

You may have listed different items for that answer, but you could
have simply said "things they are not using anymore." Even with the
sizes of houses being larger than ever and the amount of debt per
home at an all time high, Americans still don't have room for all of
the stuff that they bought and now are not using.

Take a minute to walk around your house. Write down the names
of items in the following places that you have used or worn less than
two times in the last month.

Your closet –

Under your bed –

Garage –

Trunk of your car –

How much do you think all of those items cost combined?

It is hard to justify spending money on something you will not use much, when you could save that money, use it on things you need, or use it for work in God's kingdom. Here are some practical tips for controlling spending:

1. Honestly pray about your purchases before you buy anything.
2. Learn the difference between wants and needs.
3. Create a few questions to ask yourself before making a purchase such as: Do I really need this? How much will I use it? Will it put a strain on my budget? Will it limit my giving to the church? Will it hurt my witness?
4. Be aware of cultural pressure to spend.
5. Avoid impulse buying, recreational shopping, and blues-binge spending.
6. Find an accountability partner who you can talk to about potential purchases or shopping sprees.

Write down the number for each practical tip you will try to use.

Write down three questions you will ask yourself before spending money.

Read Luke 14:28-33. What does this passage say about spending?

How does this passage relate to whole-life stewardship?

What is one area of spending you need to control?
Ask God to help you.

Go to the *Week Three Wrap-Up* on page 50 and write down the one area of spending you need to control better.

[1] U.S. Census Bureau, "Characteristics of New Housing [cited 6 November 2006]. Available from the Internet: www.census.gov/const/www/charindex. html#simglecomplete.
[2] David W. Jones, "One Man's Treasure Is Another Man's…" [cited 6 November 2006]. Available from the Internet: www.allaroundcleveland.com/site/news. cfm?newsid=17390317

day four

How to Get Out of Debt

The wicked borrows and does not repay,
But the righteous is gracious and giving. Psalm 37:21

Aren't you glad that failure isn't final? I think we love the story of the prodigal son because we can all identify with him. At some point in time or in some area of life, we have all ignored our Father's Word and have left the security of his home. But like the prodigal, when we came to our senses, we understood the vast goodness our Father had provided. It is God's grace that draws us home.

Making Change, page 83

Consider these staggering statistics about credit-card debt and use in the United States:

ᴄ⌀ Total American consumer debt reached $2.2 trillion in 2005, up from $1 trillion in 1994.

ᴄ⌀ Total American household consumer debt averaged $11,840 in 2005.

ᴄ⌀ Approximately 96 percent of Americans will have to retire financially dependent on government, family, or charity, according to a 2003 study.

ᴄ⌀ In 2005 the number of U.S. households filing for bankruptcy was 2.39 million, a 12.8 percent increase over 2004.

ᴄ⌀ According to a 2004 study, the number-one cause of divorce is financial stress.

ᴄ⌀ In 2004, 76 percent of undergraduate college students had at least one credit card in their names, with an average outstanding balance or $2,169.

ᴄ⌀ As of 2004, the average graduate student had six credit cards, and one in seven owed more that $15,000.[1]

We can learn a lot from the Jurassic Park movies of the 90's: just because we can do something, doesn't mean we should. That's a good guide for acquiring credit cards and debt.

Read Romans 13:7-8. What do these verses say about debt?

What do the verses say about whole-life stewardship?

Probably the most misused tool in the American economy is the credit card. Although it can be helpful, a quick look at it reminds us of why God warns us against going in debt when we don't have to.

Most young adults can only qualify for high-rate credit cards. Let's say a person has this type of card for instance, with 23.99 percent interest rate. If he were to charge $1,000.00 for a HDTV on his credit card, and then paid the minimum rate to the credit company, beginning at $50/month, by the time that TV was paid off six years later he would have paid almost $600 extra in interest. That doesn't count any late fees he may have paid for each time he was a few days late with a payment. If that same person would have saved their $50 a month, a year and a half later they could have bought the TV with cash, avoided wasting $570.00 over the next four and a half years, and missed out on all of the stress that comes from being in debt.

You can see how God's warning in Romans is just another way that He is looking out for our best interest, financially and emotionally.

Go to the *Week Three Wrap-Up* on page 50 and write down one idea or Scripture that stood out to you today.

---

[1] "Credit Card Industry Facts and Personal Debt Statistic" [cited 6 November 2006]. Available from the Internet: http//creditcards.com/statistics/statistics.php.

day five

How to
Save and Invest

Go to the ant, you slacker!
Observe its ways and become wise. Proverbs 6:6

Saving and investing are biblical principles, but they must be employed with biblical priorities. Saving can become hoarding if accumulating money becomes the object of our devotion. This attitude often leads to greed and stinginess. It can separate families, spoil children, and breed dishonesty.

On the other hand, saving and investing can also provide for our future needs … while making extraordinary resources available for kingdom advance.

Making Change, page 95

In the sixth century B.C. Aesop told this story of the ant and the grasshopper.

In a field one summer's day a grasshopper was hopping about, chirping and singing to its heart's content. An ant passed by, bearing along with great toil an ear of corn he was taking to the nest.

"Why not come and chat with me," said the grasshopper, "instead of toiling and moiling in that way?"

"I am helping to lay up food for the winter," said the ant, "and recommend you to do the same."

"Why bother about winter?" said the grasshopper; "we have got plenty of food at present." But the ant went on its way and continued its toil. When the winter came, the grasshopper had no food and found itself dying of hunger while it saw the ants distributing every day corn and grain from the stores they had collected in the summer. Then the grasshopper knew: it is best to prepare for the days of necessity.

From both Solomon and Aesop the ant teaches us to save.
How is your family encouraging you to save money right now?

How have your own money practices affected your attitude about saving and investing?

If you are not a saver, what is your reason for not saving?

Does saving indicate a lack of faith? Why or why not?

Read 2 Corinthians 9:8. How can saving money free you to "excel in every good work"?

Read 1 Timothy 6:6-19. What good reasons does this passage give for saving and investing?

Do a quick interview with one of your parents. Ask:
  1) What do you think the average debt maintenance is for people on your street or in your building each month?
  2) How many people on your street or in your building do you think have no credit card debt?

Take your parent's answer from question one and multiply it by twelve. How much money is that per year?

If you had that money to use for kingdom causes, what would you do with it?

Ask God to show you how you can begin to invest money right now. Also ask God to give you wisdom about applying for and using credit cards in the future.

Finish the *Week Three Wrap-Up* on the next page.

wrap-up

Day One Thought or Verse

Day Two Thought or Verse

Day Three
The one area of spending I need to control better:

Day Four Thought or Verse

Day Five Thought or Verse

As a result of this week's study, one area of my life that I need to pray more about is:

One goal I would like to set as a result of this week's study:

four

Still Giving After All These Years

1. How do sacrifice and worship relate today?

"Brothers, by the mercies of God, I urge you to present your bodies as a _____ sacrifice, holy and pleasing to God."
Romans 12:1

2. Isn't tithing just an Old Testament concept?

"Abram gave him a _____ of everything."
Genesis 14:17-20

3. How does giving relate to God's kingdom and to a Christian's place in this kingdom?

Where is your _____?

What is your _____ here?

Is your _____ priority the kingdom of God?

Therefore, brothers, by the mercies of God, I urge you to present your bodies as a living sacrifice, holy and pleasing to God; this is your spiritual worship. Do not be conformed to this age, but be transformed by the renewing of your mind, so that you may discern what is the good, pleasing, and perfect will of God.
Romans 12:1-2

four

Still Giving After All These Years

Do you know your parents' plan for giving to the church?

What factors have determined the way you give to and through the church?

How has your giving changed over time?

Turn to the viewer guide on page 51 and record your responses as you watch this week's DVD segment.

1. Sacrifice and Worship Read Romans 12:1-2.

How did Paul define sacrifice for a Christian?

How does this definition compare to Old Testament sacrifice in worship?

How does Paul's view of sacrifice relate to whole-life stewardship?

Read the following verses and note what they say about worship and sacrifice for Christians and about whole-life stewardship.

Mark 12:33

Ephesians 5:1-2

Hebrews 13:15-16

2. Tithing Read Leviticus 27:30.

According to Old Testament law, what was the legal requirement for giving to God?

Read Malachi 2:17; 3:7-10. How had the people failed in their worship of God?

How was their failure related to whole-life stewardship?

Read Matthew 22:21 and Luke 18:9-14. What did Jesus say about giving?

What did He say about whole-life stewardship?

How does the concept of going beyond the tithe relate to whole-life stewardship?

3. Kingdom Giving Read Matthew 6:9-13, 19-24.

Although the Lord's Prayer does not specifically mention giving, how can giving be tied to that prayer?

Following the Lord's Prayer, what did Jesus say about possessions?

What are the implications for giving?

Read Luke 18:18-23. How does this passage reflect Jesus' thoughts about legalistic living and giving?

Think again about your thoughts and practices of giving. Is it based more on family teaching and lifestyle choices or on biblical teaching?

Is it legalistic?

How does your giving plan relate to whole-life stewardship?

What would you like to change about your financial giving?

day
one

The King Wants You

Brothers, by the mercies of God, I urge you to present
your bodies as a living sacrifice, holy and pleasing to
God; this is your spiritual worship. Romans 12:1

Think back to the stories involving sacrifices in the Old Testament.
If you can't remember any, read Leviticus 3. Answer the following
questions about Old Testament sacrifices:

What things were sacrificed?

How were sacrifices made?

What is one reason that people made sacrifices?

In the Old Testament times, the Israelites would sacrifice the lives of
their animals to pay the penalty for their sins and to please God. The
New Testament teaches that in giving His life for our sins, Jesus was
the final and greatest sacrifice for the sins of all people. So although
we no longer need to sacrifice a life in payment for sins, God calls
us to become a living sacrifice in worshiping Him. When we seek to
worship God, not just by giving a portion, but by truly seeking His
will for every part of our lives, we please Him. That's what Paul is
referring to in Romans chapter 12.
"To present your bodies as a living sacrifice" means that we
are to offer all we are and all we possess to God for His pleasure.

List some people you know or have heard of who tried to give
everything they had to a cause (a team, a hobby, a loved one,
a nation).

What are the names of some people who tried to give everything they had for the service of God – people you might consider a "living sacrifice."

Read Hebrews 9:26; 10:10,12,14. What does this passage say about Jesus' sacrifice for you?

What, then, should you sacrifice for Him?

Does what you hear on Sunday morning and what you read in the Bible impact your daily life?

What are some ways that you have presented your body as a sacrifice to God as a result of the things you have heard in church and your Bible study over the last year?

Ask God to help you to present your life as a sacrifice to Him this week. Ask Him to show you right now several ways that your life could be more pleasing to Him. Write those ways down and pray over them.

Go to the *Week Four Wrap-Up* on page 64 and write these areas down there as well.

Thank Christ for sacrificing His life for yours on the cross.

day two

Giving Through the Ages

He blessed him and said,
"Abram is blessed by God Most High,
Creator of heaven and earth,
And give praise to God Most High
Who has handed over your enemies to you."
And Abram gave him a tenth of everything.
Genesis 14:19-20

The tithe not only recognized God's provision but also prepared Israel for further blessing. … Clearly, this is the standard and legacy of Old Testament worship.

Making Change, page 101

As early as Cain and Abel in Genesis 4, people were bringing the best and first of what they had to worship God. Genesis also records several examples of giving a tenth or a tithe. One is found in Genesis 14. In this passage, God grants Abram a great victory, enabling him to free his relatives who were taken captive and recover all of their possessions.

When Abram returned, he worshiped God and gave a tenth of all he had to Melchizedek, "a priest to God Most High" (v. 18). Notice that even in this early example the tenth was given to God's priest. It is not a stretch, then, to connect Abram's action with the later practice of bringing tithes and offerings to the tabernacle or temple. The precedent has already been set.

Another example of tithing is found in Genesis 28. Turn to it and read verses 12-22 about Jacob.

What does God promise Jacob in verse 13?

What about in verse 14? 15?

How did Jacob respond to God's promise?

What did Jacob promise to God in the last half of verse 22?

One important thing to notice about these stories is that they occurred before God gave the "ten commandments" and the law to His people. Jacob and Abram willingly gave one tenth of all they had back to the Lord. Giving to God a tenth of what He has given to His people is an ancient way of acknowledging God as our Source and worshiping Him.

What's the tithe?

the tithe = _____ of what God gave to his people that they brought back to their temple or local priests

What do you do with your tithes and offerings?

Have you begun to give one tenth of all that you take in each week back to your local church?

Ask God to help you to be aware of everything He gives you this week. As He brings these things to your attention, begin to calculate how you can bring a tithe of His provision to your local church.

Go to the *Week Four Wrap-Up* on page 64 and write one Scripture or thought that spoke to you from today's study.

day three

Jesus on Tithing

Woe to you, scribes and Pharisees, hypocrites! You pay a tenth of mint, dill, and cumin, yet you have neglected the more important matters of the law – justice, mercy, and faith. These things should have been done without neglecting the others. Matthew 23:23

Young couples in a Sunday School class were having a lively discussion about God as the Source of all they are and have, when the teacher asked whether anyone would like to give a testimony on tithing. One couple admitted that they tithed, and they were quickly challenged by the others in the class.

"You mean you actually give away 10 percent of what you earn?"

Affirmative.

"But that includes all you give to all charities, right?"

Negative.

"You mean you really give 10 percent to the church? But that includes missions giving and building program gifts, right?"

Nope.

The couple went on to explain that giving was a joy for them and that while giving the tithe as their regular, basic offering to the church had become routine for them, they also found real joy in giving other offerings for specific causes above the tithe. They pointed out that according to Malachi 3:10, the tithe is the Lord's, and it is to be given to the church.

This young couple had learned early in life that everything they had was God's and He had blessed them abundantly. They were thankful and wanted to honor God with their gifts as well as with their lifestyle.

Read Matthew 5:17. Do you think these words include tithing?

How do you think they apply to the church today?

You read Matthew 23:23 at the beginning of today's study. What does the last sentence of this verse mean?

In verse 23, Jesus was making the point that the Pharisees should give their tithes, as well as being just and merciful toward others and faithful toward God. They should not choose one or the other.

In this verse, Jesus was clearly correcting the Pharisees for their actions. Who do you think Jesus would correct in our churches today? Why?

Stop and Listen

If Jesus spoke to you directly about one area of worship or lifestyle that you need to correct, what habit would He target?

Take a few minutes to talk to God about that area. Thank Him for His forgiveness of your sins in that area. Ask Him to give you strength to be like Him in that regard.

If you occasionally give money to the church to make up for sinful habits, talk to God about that. Let Him know that your new desire is to please Him with your tithes and in the other areas of your life, not just one or the other.

Go to the *Week Four Wrap-Up* on page 64 and write one Scripture or thought that spoke to you from today's study.

day
four

Open the Floodgates

"Bring the full 10 percent into the storehouse so that there may be food in My house. Test Me in this way," says the Lord of Hosts. "See if I will not open the floodgates of heaven and pour out on you a blessing for you without measure." Malachi 3:10

God's heartbeat to open the windows, pour out blessing, and rebuke the devourer has to do with his singular passion – that he be known as King among all the nations. (*Making Change*, page 113) The purpose of God's promise in Malachi 3 wasn't to give us a formula of how we can get rich quick. Even if God decides to do that for us, it is about something bigger than that. We can never forget that we receive blessings from Him so that we can in turn bless others, to further our role in God's great and glorious kingdom work.

Do you remember that TV commercial that showed parents giving a new car to their daughter, who quickly freaked out (in a bad way) because she wanted a car that was a different color?

That is similar to what Malachi said God's people were doing with their relationship with God. They were so accustomed to God's gracious gifts that they had forgotten to acknowledge and thank Him. Their worship had become complacent. They no longer gave God their best. Does any of that sound similar to the way we act toward God today?

When Malachi challenged the people about their behavior, they asked, "How have we wearied Him?" (Mal. 2:17) and "How do we rob You?" (Mal. 3:8). After confronting the people about this, God told them that if they returned to authentic worship, bringing the full tithe, He would pour out blessings on them. This is just one more reminder that God wants to bless His children. But too often people in Malachi's day, as well as our own, see the tithe as a penalty rather than a privilege, an obligation rather than an act of worship.

If you get a moment this week, read through the entire book of Malachi. (It is incredibly short!) Notice that in Malachi the problem was not limited to their withholding the tithe. They were also sacrificing inferior animals (see 1:7-8), giving poor instruction and causing others to stumble (see 2:8), and treating their wives with disrespect (see 2:14-16).

What does Malachi indicate that God wanted the people to do?

How does Malachi's message relate to whole-life stewardship (honoring God with every area of my life)?

Have you ever taken your Heavenly Father's love for granted?

What have you done or what will you do to find joy in that relationship again?

Take a few minutes to talk to God about this.

Go to the *Week Four Wrap-Up* on page 64 and write one Scripture or thought that spoke to you from today's study.

day five

Living in the
Kingdom Zone

Seek first the kingdom of God and His righteousness,
and all these things will be provided for you.
Matthew 6:33

We have been called to a supernatural work that
requires us to rely on the Holy Spirit and employ all of
God's resources with His heartbeat in mind.

We must learn to live in the kingdom zone because we are
God's resources to accomplish his kingdom purposes.

Making Change, page 116

Open up your Bible to Exodus 19 and read verses 4-6.

How does God refer to His people in verse 5?

Nomadic people, like the Israelites, were always moving. Because of
this, they always had their most precious possessions with them. They
may have had precious stones or pieces of gold, which they kept in
a bag hidden in their garments or even sewn into the clothes they
wore. These possessions were so highly prized that the owner never
wanted to be separate from them. That's the kind of relationship God
was talking about in this passage. When He called the Israelites his
"treasured possession," God was saying, "Even though I already
own everything, I have chosen this nation as My most treasured
people."

God also said that He expected the people to listen to Him and
to obey Him. God expected three things from His chosen people:
to embody [or represent] His name, to embrace His mission [point
people to Him], and to obey His word.[1] In the New Testament,
the Lord's Prayer picks up on these same three themes. It is truly a
kingdom message that runs throughout the Bible, connecting God
with His people, His special treasure.

How does knowing that you are loved by God as His special treasure
make you feel?

Open up your Bible to Matthew 6. Read verses 9-13.
How does the Lord's Prayer convey God's desire that His people embody His name, embrace His mission, and obey His Word?

Look at Matthew 6:19-20. In light of the three things God wants His people to do, how can you lay up treasure in Heaven?

Now read Matthew 6:24. How does serving money keep a person from serving God?

God has chosen to do His work on earth through His people, His special treasure. How are you embodying His name, embracing His mission, and obeying His Word?

How does the way you spend your money give evidence of what you are doing for the kingdom of God?

How does the way you spend your time give evidence of this?

Spend a few minutes talking to God about using your time and your money for the glory of His kingdom.

Go to the *Week Four Wrap-Up* on page 64 and write one Scripture or thought that spoke to you from today's study.

[1] To learn more about Empowering Kingdom Growth, see Ken Hemphill, EKG: The Heartbeat of God (Nashville: Broadman & Holman, 2004)

wrap-up

Day One
Ways my life can be more sacrificial and pleasing to God:

Day Two Thought or Verse

Day Three Thought or Verse

Day Four Thought or Verse

Day Five Thought or Verse

As a result of this week's study, one area of my life that I need to pray more about is:

One goal I would like to set as a result of this week's study:

Good Reasons To Be A Giver

1. What does the New Testament say about how we should give?

   The Law of _____

   The Law of _____ Giving

   The Law of _____

   The Law of _____

2. Does attitude matter?

   "God loves a _____ giver." 2 Corinthians 9:7

3. What happens when we give?

   Giving _____ us.

   Giving produces _____ to God.

   Giving meets _____.

   Giving glorifies _____.

   How is the Southern Baptist Cooperative Program an example of Paul's teaching about giving?

The person who sows sparingly will also reap sparingly, and the person who sows generously will also reap generously. Each person should do as he has decided in his heart—not out of regret or out of necessity, for God loves a cheerful giver. 2 Corinthians 9:6-7

Good Reasons To Be A Giver

Review what you learned in this week's daily Bible studies.

What did you learn it means to be a "living sacrifice?"

What did you learn about tithing?

What do you think it means to live in a "Kingdom Zone?"

Turn to the viewer guide on page 65 and record your responses as you watch this week's DVD segment.

1. A New Testament Model for Giving Read 1 Corinthians 16:1-2.

When and how much did Paul say these churchgoers should give?

How do you think these verses apply today regarding frequency and amount?

Read 2 Corinthians 8:1-7. What does grace mean?

How are grace and giving related in this passage?

Have you ever known anyone who gave with grace? How would you describe that person's giving?

Some churches are also known for their grace of giving. How would you describe such a church? What is needed for your church to be known for its grace giving?

2. Attitude Read 2 Corinthians 9:7.

Do you think most people give gladly or reluctantly? Why?

Are grace, generosity, and joy connected? If so, in what ways?

3. Results of Giving Read 2 Corinthians 9:10-15.

Does giving have a bigger impact on the giver or the one who receives?

What happens to the giver's relationship with God?

Read Malachi 2:17; 3:7-10. How had the people failed in their worship?

How was their future related to whole-life stewardship?

Read Matt. 23:23 and Luke 18:9-14. What was Jesus saying about whole-life stewardship? How does the concept of going beyond the tithe relate to whole-life stewardship?

4. Corporate Giving Read 1 Corinthians 16:1-5; 2 Corinthians 8:1-5; 9:10-15; Philippians 4:15-20.

What is the impact on the kingdom when Christians and churches work together to give?

What are some examples you know of where churches worked together to bring glory to God and meet the needs of others?

5. Your Giving

How do you measure up to Paul's standards for giving?

If you could make a small change in giving, what would you change?
   ___ The amount you give
   ___ Your plan for giving
   ___ The frequency and regularity of your giving
   ___ Your attitude in giving

Developing Consistency

On the first day of the week, each of you is to set
something aside and save to the extent that he
prospers, so that no collections will need to be made
when I come. 1 Corinthians 16:2

All we do is "the Lord's work." This sounds impossible
and highly impractical in one sense, and yet it is cer-
tainly true. We have been guilty of compartmentalizing
our life in terms of sacred and secular. But for the kingdom citizen, nothing is secular. Every aspect of our life
comes under the sovereign rule of the King, …
Every kingdom citizen is called, gifted, and empowered for
ministry. There are no kingdom spectators.

Making Change, pages 122-23

A high school student sat down with her stay-at-home mom to fill
out applications for college scholarships. One blank was for the
annual household income. With just a little figuring the student
wrote down an amount while her mom looked on in amazement.
"How did you know your dad's annual income?"

The daughter smiled and said, "Every Saturday night Daddy
places Bibles, Sunday School books, and offering envelopes for the
two of you near the front door so that they are ready to pick up on
Sunday morning. It's no secret that Daddy believes in tithing. There
on your Bibles are two offering envelopes with the same amount for
each of you."

Looking back at the scholarship form, she said, "Filling in this
blank is easy. I've known Daddy's annual income since I learned to
add and multiply." This father's example had taught his family to give
with consistency.

How was the daughter in this story able to figure out how much her
father made in a year?

What do your habits say about your role in the kingdom?

Read again 1 Corinthians 16:2. Who was included in Paul's expectation to give?

How did people determine how much to give?

Paul taught all the people to give consistently and proportionately. How does his teaching apply to you today?

Do you think all of your life belongs to God? What part of your life have you tried to segment for yourself or away from God?

Go to the *Week Five Wrap-Up* on page 78 and write one Scripture or thought that spoke to you from today's study.

day two

The Grace of Giving

During a severe testing by affliction, their abundance of joy and their deep poverty overflowed into the wealth of their generosity. 2 Corinthians 8:2

> I have always found it curious that people with little means are often more generous than those with great abundance. Does accumulation of wealth make us more dependent on wealth for our security? *Making Change*, page 128

A widow lived with her teenage daughters in a rural community. Even by the modest standards of the area, they had little, but then they didn't need a lot. They had a roof over their heads, even if it did leak sometimes. They had one another, their friends, and, of course, the church.

At the end of a mid-November sermon, the pastor made an announcement: "The deacons met this past week and decided they want the church to take a special offering in a few weeks to help a poor family in our community. I wanted to let you know so that you could begin planning for that opportunity to help others in our neighborhood."

The female family went home from church excited about preparations for the holidays. Over lunch they talked about the special offering and what they could do to help. The younger daughter said, "Mr. Wall told me that I could work some extra hours at his store during our Thanksgiving and Christmas school breaks. He'll probably also give me a discount on any gifts I buy there, so I can give that money to the offering." The older daughter added, "I've been saving all year for a new holiday dress, but I saw one I really like at the secondhand store that costs a lot less. I can give that money." The mother, pleased with her daughters' generosity, added, "If we cut back just a little on our food budget, we can give that money too." Since they all loved a mac-and-cheese meal anyway, both girls thought this was a good idea.

The Saturday before the offering at church, they pooled and counted their money. It came to $55.27—not much, but they hoped it would help the needy family in their neighborhood.

The following Thursday night they were surprised to see the pastor at their door. He reminded them of the special offering the church had taken. He was pleased to present them a check for $60. He hoped it would make their Christmas more festive.

Read Luke 21:1-4. Who was the most blessed in their giving, the rich people or the widow? Why?

In the story you just read about the mother and daughters, who in the church was most blessed by this family's giving? Do you think this family felt more blessed in giving or in receiving?

What do these two stories teach about grace giving and proportional giving?

Read Matthew 10:8 and Acts 20:35. When have you felt blessed in your giving?

Go to the *Week Five Wrap-Up* on page 78 and write one Scripture or thought that spoke to you from today's study.

day
three

The Laws of Giving

Remember this: the person who sows sparingly will also reap sparingly, and the person who sows generously will also reap generously. 2 Corinthians 9:6

The word translated "generous gift" in 2 Corinthians 9:5 is from the Greek word eulogia. Sound familiar? Not many people would describe an offering as a eulogy, but our giving is always a blessing to others. We often pray that God will bless someone, but we forget that we can also bestow a blessing on them by our own actions of giving.

If you want God to bless the poor, [then you] give to the poor.

If you want Him to bless the missionaries, give to missions causes. *Making Change*, page 135

As Peter and John approached the temple complex, they saw a man who was born lame begging for money. He was there every day asking people to help him. He'd been coming there so long he was a fixture. He was an inconvenience to almost anyone who walked by him. He knew they hardly looked at him, and if they did, their stares carried pity or disdain.

But Peter and John saw the man. They didn't toss in a few coins to ease their conscience. No, they stopped and addressed the man: "Look at us." When he had the man's full attention, Peter said, "I have neither silver nor gold, but what I have, I give to you: In the name of Jesus Christ the Nazarene, get up and walk!"

Then Peter took the man's hand and helped him to his feet. He felt his knees shake, then strengthen. He couldn't believe it! Overcome with joy, he felt like shouting. Leaping, he entered the temple, praising God. People saw him and were amazed, and they too worshiped and praised God.

Read this account in Acts 3:1-10. Which would have been easier for Peter and John—to give the man a little money or to ask God to heal him?

How was their gift a witness to God?

What results do you think followed? The biblical account identifies some results. What else might have happened?

Who was blessed because of this generous gift?

What was the kingdom impact of this gift?

Which is easier—to give a little money or to give time and ability to meet a need or solve a problem? Does doing one mean that you do not need to do the other?

Go to the *Week Five Wrap-Up* on page 78 and write one Scripture or thought that spoke to you from today's study.

day four

A Strategy for Cooperative Giving

"Macedonia and Achaia were pleased to make contributions to the poor among the saints in Jerusalem." Romans 15:26

Historically, one of the toughest places to witness in America has been New Orleans. That has changed since the hurricanes hit in 2005. Church groups who have been taking mission trips to New Orleans for some time have had completely different experiences on their post-Katrina trips: "People have heard about Southern Baptists," remarked one volunteer, "and what they've heard is good. They have eaten Southern Baptist meals, drunk water provided by Southern Baptists, or had their houses rebuilt by Baptist teams. Now they're ready to hear about the Jesus those Baptist teams serve."

Because Baptist have given generously and collaboratively and because they have volunteered their time to prepare and go when disaster hits, people's needs have been met, God's name has been glorified, and more people have entered the kingdom. That's what cooperative giving is all about. Cooperating with other churches by putting our funds and efforts and skills together to make the biggest impact possible for the kingdom.

Take a moment to look at the example set by the church in Macedonia. Read through 2 Corinthians chapter 8. Beside each set of verses below, write down an idea or principle that we can apply to cooperative giving today.

2 Corinthians 8:1-4

2 Corinthians 8:7

2 Corinthians 8:8-9

74

2 Corinthians 8:12

2 Corinthians 8:13-15

2 Corinthians 8:24

What has been your church's experience in cooperative giving?

Have you given to any special, cooperative giving campaigns?

Try to find out this week how much of each dollar you give to the church is set aside for cooperative plans that reach outside of your local church.

Go to the *Week Five Wrap-Up* on page 78 and write one Scripture or thought that spoke to you from today's study.

Spend a few minutes thanking God for the church you attend. Thank Him for the ways He has used your church in the past to bless other churches. Thank Him for letting your church team with other churches to make a greater impact for His glory.

To learn more about some of the work that results from cooperative giving, go to www.namb.net (the North American Mission Board).

day five

The Results of Giving

The ministry of this service is not only supplying the needs of the saints, but is also overflowing in many acts of thanksgiving to God. 2 Corinthians 9:12

Life really isn't about us. We live to give glory and thanksgiving to God, and living with generosity provides us the opportunity to do just that.   *Making Change*, page 141

Think of the popular shows on TV right now. Take one minute and write down the titles of shows where most of the main characters are trying to get rich (or richer).

Now take one minute and write down the titles of every show where there are characters who are trying to become more poor.

Being in the middle of God's will for your life doesn't mean you'll definitely end up rich. It may mean that you'll be on a tight budget the rest of your life. It definitely means that, no matter what your financial situation is, there will always be someone with greater needs than you and, there will always be a way you can help others in need.

Look back at 2 Corinthians 8:2 again. What does this verse say about the financial state of the Christians in Macedonia?

What reasons and results of giving can we see in the following verses:

2 Corinthians 8:2

2 Corinthians 9:8-9

2 Corinthians 9:10-15

Proverbs 11:25

Proverbs 19:17

Luke 6:38

What motivates you to give? Can you think of any blessings you have received already from giving?

Take a few minutes to talk to God. Ask Him to show you new ways that He may want you to give. Ask Him to help you to give out of right motives -- to glorify Him, to help others – not just for how He might reward you.

What is one verse that spoke to you in this week of Bible study?

What is one thought or idea that stuck with you from this week?

On the next page, complete the *Week Five Wrap-Up*.

wrap-up

Day One
Ways my life can be more sacrificial and pleasing to God:

Day Two Thought or Verse

Day Three Thought or Verse

Day Four Thought or Verse

Day Five Thought or Verse

As a result of this week's study, one area of my life that I need to pray more about is:

One goal I would like to set as a result of this week's study:

six

Compounding Interest and Kingdom Cooperation

1. What's giving got to do with going?

   "How can they hear without a _____?"
   Romans 10:14

2. What can we do?

   We can _____.

   Get your _____ house in order?

   Begin a _____ savings account.

   Learn to share your _____.

   Consider a _____ trip.

3. What can our church do?

   Create a _____.

   Increase _____ to all four quadrants.

   _____ with others.

   How can stewardship help us grow as Christians?

   How can they call on Him in whom they have not believed? And how can they believe without hearing about Him? And how can they hear without a preacher? And how can they preach unless they are sent?
   Romans 10:14-15

six
Compounding Interest and Kingdom Cooperation

Share with the group one meaningful lesson or Scripture from this past week's daily Bible studies. If you feel comfortable, share one goal you set or prayer you began praying this past week.

What projects have you worked on in your church that required both volunteer time and financial support? Do members of your church go on mission trips? Who goes? How are the trips funded?

What is a bigger sacrifice for you – giving your time or your money?

What needs compel you to give both your time and your money?

Turn to the viewer guide on page 79 and record your responses as you watch this week's DVD segment.

1. Giving and Going Read Romans 10:1,9-15.

What is the message we seek to proclaim by our giving and going?

To whom are we to carry the message?

Who is responsible for carrying the message?

Read Matthew 28:18-20 and Acts 1:8. By whose power and authority are we commissioned?

What are we to do? Where are we to go? Where do we begin?

2. My Responsibility

As a result of this study, what is your goal for managing your finances?

As a result of this study, what is your goal for giving?

As a result of this study, what is your goal for giving your time?

3. Our Church's Responsibility Read Acts 1:8.

What is your church doing to reach your community?

What is your church doing to reach your state?

What is your church doing to reach North America?

What is your church doing to reach the world?

How does your church budget and activities reflect these areas?

How can your youth ministry be more active in each area?

4. Stewardship and Personal Growth Read Romans 10:16-18.

You are a Christian today because people gave their time and money so that you could hear the good news of Jesus Christ.

Who gave their time? Their money?

Who has discipled you?

How has this study affected your personal faith journey?

How will it impact your stewardship of all your resources?

Read 1 Corinthians 3:9-16. How are church members to work together? For what purpose?

What difference does one person make?

What is your contribution to kingdom building?

First and Last Words

You will receive power when the Holy Spirit has come
upon you, and you will be My witnesses in Jerusalem,
in all Judea and Samaria, and to the ends
of the earth. Acts 1:8

The kingdom. First and last. And everything in between.
That was Jesus' message to the people of his day. It remains
his heartbeat to us even now.   *Making Change*, page 154

George is consumed by school work. He doesn't take time for anything else. He gets up early every morning to review notes for any
pop quiz he might have that day. He takes down every note given
by every teacher in every class. He comes home after school, takes a
short break for a snack, and then hits the books until it's time
for bed.

Jessica is obsessed with fitness. She's always on the move to burn
those carbs, develop her abs, and keep the pounds off. She knows the
food value of every bite she puts in her mouth. And she freely shares
her passion with everyone around her. Let's go running! Time for
aerobics! Put down that doughnut!

Rusty is a sports nut. He can tell you this week's college and pro
sports lineup and all the stats. Punch him in the middle of the night,
and he can quote last week's scores and next week's match-ups. If he's
not at a game or watching one on TV, then he's reading about it in
a magazine or figuring out what player to start in his on-line fantasy
league. Sports are his life.

Joy is really into clothes. Really, really! In class, she's usually
reading this month's edition of Cosmo-girl. Every day after school
she hits the mall to try on the newest lines at Hollister, Forever 21,
and any new stores that have just opened up. At night, it's time to get
on-line to check out all the newest styles from New York, L.A., and
around the world.

OK, most people are not quite this focused. But Jesus was. He
started talking about the kingdom of God in His first sermon, and
He was still talking about it as He prepared to leave earth and return
to heaven. Jesus was all about the kingdom because He knew it was

His Father's will that people embrace His name, embody His mission, and obey His word—all kingdom work.

He wants the kingdom to be your passion and to shape the way you see the world you live in.

Read Exodus 19:5-6. What message did God want Moses to deliver to the Hebrew people after He delivered them from slavery in Egypt?

Read Matthew 4:17,23. Right after His temptation Jesus began to preach about the kingdom. How are temptation and kingdom focus related in your life?

Read Matthew 5:3,10,19-20; 6:10,33; 7:13,21. These verses present Jesus' teaching on the kingdom in the Sermon on the Mount. How does the kingdom of God provide a framework for Jesus' message?

How does the kingdom of heaven provide a framework for your life?

If we put your story on the previous page, what would people identify as your passion, your worldview, the single focus that shapes your life?

Turn to the *Week Six Wrap-Up* on page 92. Write down one Scripture or idea that resonated with you today.

Spend a few minutes praying. Ask God to remind you of the following question when you make decisions about life this week: How could this decision best impact others for eternity in God's kingdom?

A Living Model of
Cooperative Missions

Go therefore, and make disciples of all nations,
baptizing them in the name of the Father and of the
Son and of the Holy Spirit. Matthew 28:19

In the next sentence fill in blanks 1-3 the following way: blank 1
– your hometown; blank 2 – your county (or parish); blank 3 – your
country.

You will be My witnesses in 1)_____, 2) _____
_____, throughout 3) _____, and to the ends of the
earth.

If Jesus popped in on your church today and restated Acts 1:8 for
your congregation, that might be His charge to you.

> "Discipling the nations is a command of God, not a
> suggestion. It would be easy to see it as an impossible task if
> it weren't for the promise of the risen Lord that He would be
> with us as we go."   *Making Change*, page 160

God's Word assures us that the resources are available for us to
complete this task before the King returns. If we are going to
complete this task, our local churches must be intentional, globally
focused, and cooperative. The task demands that each church form
partnerships with like-minded churches for the sake of the kingdom.
Cooperation is key!

Good Samaritan Ministries (GSM) is the heartbeat of Brownwood,
Texas. Since 1993, Good Samaritan has been meeting the needs of
people in the heartland of Texas. Angelia Bostic, the center's director,
reports that volunteers are key to everything Good Samaritan does.
Good Samaritan operates these ministries:

School supplies. Sunday School classes and church groups make
special donations to defray the cost of school supplies that GSM
supplies for about 200 students.

Food Pantry. Area churches and groups collect food items and special donations for the pantry. During any month, between 90 and 120 different volunteers serve in the food pantry alone.

Clothing. The generous contributions of area residents and churches make the items in the clothing store available to anyone who wants to shop there.

Financial Assistance. GSM provides limited financial assistance to residents of Brown County under two programs. Through Help for Health individuals can receive help with prescriptions, doctor visits, dental visits, eyeglasses, and eye exams. Through Samaritan Aid families can receive assistance with utility and rent bills.

Personal and spiritual help. Employees and volunteers always offer a listening ear, a caring heart, and a Christian witness. New Testaments and tracts are always available. Even preschoolers help by drawing pictures to be given with the tracts and New Testaments.

GSM receives some support from the North American Mission Board, but churches and individuals in and around Brownwood primarily support the work. GSM benefits from volunteers from preschoolers through senior adults, and help comes from more than 40 area churches representing different races, languages, and denominations – Christians coming together to meet a variety of needs, all in the name of Jesus. Sounds a lot like God's kingdom, doesn't it?

You can learn more about GSM at *www.goodsambwd.org.*

Read Acts 1:8 again. How is GSM's ministry an example of all four areas in Jesus' mandate?

What opportunities like GSM are available in your area for giving and going in Jesus' name?

Write those areas on the *Week Six Wrap-Up* on page 92 under "Day Two." Spend a few minutes praying for those ministries and asking God to show you how you can be involved in them in the next month.

day three

The Mutual Fund of Missions

> On the first day of the week, each of you is to set something aside and save to the extent that he prospers, so that no collections will need to be made when I come. 1 Corinthians 16:2

How can the small amount of my tithes and offering make a difference for the kingdom of God? How can our church really impact Jerusalem, Judea, Samaria, and the ends of the earth? What's the best way to ensure that our money is maximized and used well in authentic missions endeavors? How do we know which places to invest our support with so many worthy options to choose from?

These are serious questions to ask because the King is serious about getting his resources in the hands of people who will join him in reaching the nations.

Making Change, pages 168-169

You may remember the Jim Carrey movie Fun with Dick and Jane (2005). Dick and Jane are living the good life. He's just gotten a big promotion and convinced his wife to quit her job. Then suddenly everything changes. His company goes under, and he loses his job. Dick tries, but can't get a job anywhere. Desperate to keep their home and maintain their lifestyle and their image among their friends, they resort to a life of crime and steal from others, including Dick's former boss.

Although the movie may have been funny, we hear similar real life stories all too often. Companies like Enron appeared to be thriving, attract investors, and then fall apart. As a result, people lose their jobs, their savings, their retirement, and their financial peace of mind.

This may have happened to your family. We've looked in past weeks at Scriptures that talk about investing, so we know that is important to God.

We also, however, need to let these stories remind us that earthly treasures do fail us. In contrast, treasures we lay up in heaven are eternal. They will not fail because we can trust the One who holds them in His care.

Sometimes investing in earthly ways provides a plan for us to support kingdom goals. Do you have plans for your savings and investments? What are they?

Do they include kingdom causes? In what way?

In addition to the 10% of your income you give to the church, start praying about putting a little extra money aside each month in a "kingdom" account. This account would be something you would use in special cases when God gives you the opportunity to give or to go somewhere to serve to meet the needs of others. At the end of this week, try to decide on an amount of money (or percent of your income) that you will try to set aside each month for this kingdom account. When you decide on it, write it on the *Week Six Wrap-Up* under "Day 3." How does your budget reflect kingdom causes?

If you attend a Southern Baptist Church and you are giving a tithe to it, here is how your money that is sent to the Southern Baptist Convention is used for the kingdom:

*50% – International Mission Board; 22.79% - North American Mission Board; 21.64% - seminaries for training ministers; 1.49% - Ethics and Religious Liberty Commission; .76% - Guidestone Financial Services for ministerial relief; 3.32% - SBC operating budget.

* In other words, 94.43 percent of the money your church sends to the SBC goes directly to training ministers and supporting missionaries.

Read Matthew 6:19-21. Where is your storehouse?

What treasure are you collecting?

Spend some time praying that God will help you to understand the best way to use and invest the gifts and resources He has given to you.

day four

Revealed by Fire

If anyone builds on the foundation with gold, silver, costly stones, wood, hay or straw, each one's work will become obvious, for the day will disclose it, because it will be revealed by fire; the fire will test the quality of each one's work. 1 Corinthians 3:12-13

If you currently or ever played on any kind of athletic team, you can appreciate the necessity of coaches. A good coach can encourage a player who is struggling, and keep a player who is hot to keep working to be even better. A good coach can help individual players put their personal desires to the side and change the way they think and play for the good of the team. A good coach can motivate you to reach individual and team goals you never thought possible.

In a way, that coaching process describes our journey as Christians: we seek to align our desires, goals and plans more closely with the King of kings. We do this so that He can help us get the most out of our time and money and efforts, like the Scripture at the top of the page teaches. We do it so that we may become valuable servants, develop a better relationship with God and others, and reach more people for Him. To reach these goals, we have to draw close to our King so that He can give us the instruction, encouragement, strength and resources we need.

Jesus' parable of the talents in Matthew 25 illustrates the Christian journey. Turn in your Bible to this chapter and read tverses 14-30.

In light of your growing understanding of God's kingdom and our role as stewards, what new insights do you have about this parable?

Below is a list of some simple ways you can invest your money today. Remember, the better we invest, the more we will have to use for kingdom work.

Savings account
> Benefits – usually will have no limit on number of transactions
> Drawbacks – lowest interest rates

Money market account – a type of savings account
>   Benefits – interest rates are better than savings acct.
>   Drawback – minimum balance usually $1,000.00 or more

CD – Certificate of Deposit
>   Benefits – higher interest rates than savings and most money markets
>   Drawbacks – withdrawal before maturity date results in a fine

A great rule that money experts live by is the 80-10-10 rule. This rule states that, at the very most, we should only spend 80% of the money we bring in each month. Then we should invest at least 10% and give at least 10% to the church. Out of the three investment opportunities you just read about, is there one you think you can begin to start putting money into? How much could you put in a month?

In addition to money, what else has God given that might be viewed in this way?

This parable was dealing specifically with managing money, so it is a great reminder that God wants us to be wise in how we spend, invest, and give our money. However, the same principles can be applied to our gifts, talents, and other possessions. We should examine each area of our life to make sure we are not missing out on chances to bring God glory and point others to Him.

What has God given you? Are you using or burying what He has given you?

What changes can you make in order to use what God has provided for kingdom purposes?

Spend some time praying about these changes. Then write them down on the *Week Six Wrap-Up* page 92.

day five

A Kingdom Celebration

Since we are receiving a kingdom that cannot be shaken, let us hold on to grace. By it, we may serve God acceptably, with reverence and awe. Hebrews 12:28

Are you beginning to understand why Christ loves the church? Are you beginning to see what is at stake? Yes, I am talking about your church—the church you attend each Sunday. Your church is crucial to the work of the King until he returns. It can and must play a pivotal role in the reaching of your Jerusalem, Judea, Samaria, and the ends of the earth. You must think strategically in all these areas and learn to give of yourself and your material resources joyously and sacrificially to advance his kingdom until he comes.

God has created the world with resources sufficient for the advance of the gospel to the ends of the earth. And he has given a portion of those resources to you in stewardship, allowing you the privilege of participation in the greatest event in time and eternity—the coming of his kingdom. It is indeed a grand joy and responsibility we share. And nothing compares with it!   *Making Change*, page 183

Just before Thanksgiving in 2006, consumers lined up for hours—even overnight—to buy the new Playstation III. Although 400,000 were available for distribution, they were in unbelievably short supply. Many of those waiting to buy the new entertainment system weren't getting it for themselves or their children for Christmas. Rather, they wanted to resell it online for more than double what they paid for it. When stores finally opened their doors, stampedes resulted.

Following Hurricanes Katrina and Rita in 2005, gas prices in the United States soared to record levels. Damage to refineries along the Gulf Coast, combined with rising world demand for oil, resulted in limited supplies of petroleum products.

Around the world are billions of people who need to know about Jesus. Most of the unreached people in our world live in a rectangular-shaped window that extends from west Africa to east Asia, from 10 degrees north to 40 degrees north of the equator. This specific region, which has increasingly become known as the 10/40 Window, encompasses the majority of the world's Muslims, Hindus, and Buddhists—billions of spiritually impoverished souls. They need the Gospel. But the Gospel isn't in short supply.

The world sometimes faces shortages in what people need and want (like gas and Playstations). But the resources needed to reach the world for Christ are already available. God owns everything, and He is faithful in supplying what we need. It is up to us, His children and stewards, to make available the resources to do what He is calling us to do.

The need for people to hear about Christ is great. The need is now.

Read Acts 16:9-10. What was God calling Paul to do in this vision?

How is God calling you to respond at this moment in your life?

God sometimes gives visions or speaks directly to call people in specific ways, but He speaks to all of us through His Word, the Bible.

What new insights have you gained in this study about what God wants you to do?

Turn to the next page for the *Week Six Wrap-Up* and complete it.

wrap-up

Day One Thought or Verse

Day Two
Local opportunities where I could give and go:

Day Three
How much money could you set aside per month (outside of your tithe) to put into your own Kingdom Fund? This fund would be set aside for times when God may impress you to give or to go somewhere to serve others. I can put _____ per month into a separate kingdom account.

Day Four
Changes I can make to use what God has provided me for His purposes:

Day Five
One thought or verse that spoke to me today:

As a result of this week's study, one area of my life that I need to pray more about is:

One goal I would like to set as a result of this week's study:

Commitment
and Celebration

Is it worth it? And will it work?

> "They said with a loud voice:
> The _____ who was slaughtered is worthy
> to receive power and riches
> and wisdom and strength
> and honor and glory and blessing!"
> Revelation 5:12

Don't collect for yourselves treasures on earth, where moth and rust destroy and where thieves break in and steal. But collect for yourself treasures in heaven, where neither moth nor rust destroys, and where thieves don't break in and steal. For where your treasure is, there your heart will be also. Matthew 6:19-21

Commitment
and Celebration

How will your life change as a result of what you have learned during this study?

What new thoughts do you have about stewardship?

What are your personal goals in the following areas:

Investing money –

Giving to my local church –

Serving others in my school and community –

Nationwide Missions –

Global Missions—

Sharing my faith –

Other –

What can your youth group and/or small group do?

What would you like your church to do?

Turn to the viewer guide on page 93 and record your responses as you watch this week's DVD segment.

Read Matthew 6:33.

What area some practical ways you can seek God's kingdom?

What are some ways members of your church can work together to seek God's kingdom?

Read Hebrews 12:1-2.

Why do we seek God's kingdom?

Read Hebrews 12:25-29.

What will be shaken and destroyed?

What will endure?

How can we be a part of what lasts forever?

Read Revelation 5:8-10.

Who is worthy to open the scroll and why?

Who are the redeemed?

Compare Revelation 5:10 with Exodus 19:5-6.

As one of God's chosen, what is your role in redeeming the nations?

Read Malachi 3:10.

In what ways has God already proven His love for you?

Write a prayer here, thanking God for His provision, protection, and presence. State in your prayer any new commitments to Him.

prayer Close in prayer together, lifting up the goals and commitments you have talked about today and over the course of this study.

Check out these additional *Making Change* Resources

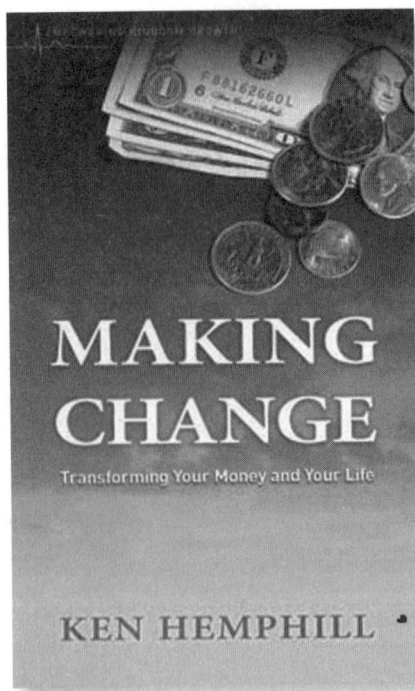